Lesson Book

Piano

Willard A. Palmer ▪ Morton Manus ▪ Amanda Vick Lethco

Additional Pages: Andrew Higgins
Additional Artwork/Engraving: Oliver Wood
Additional Proofing: Leonie McCaughren
Cover Design: Holly Fraser

Produced by
Alfred Publishing Co. (UK) Ltd.
Burnt Mill, Elizabeth Way,
Harlow
Essex, CM20 2HX

alfreduk.com

ISBN-10: 1-4706-1306-9
ISBN-13: 978-1-4706-1306-8

Cover and Interior Illustrations by David Silverman (Painted by Cheryl Hennigar)

A Note to Parents

Dear Parents,

You have a right to be proud!

Giving your child music lessons shows foresight as well as the appreciation of a fine art.

Music is a language understood by people of all nations. It is one of the most basic mediums of expression. Improved co-ordination, a broadening of interests, a discovery of the importance of self-discipline, and a world of pleasure are just a few of the rewards pupils receive.

Parents must play an important role in guiding their children's musical training. One question asked by almost all parents is, "How long should my child practise?" Later, it will be important that your child practises a specified amount. For now, the length of time is not so important, as long as they practise their assignments SEVERAL TIMES each day.

REGULAR PRACTISE IS IMPORTANT. Let your child select a regular time for practise to begin. Then, with your help, good practising habits can be established. Your child's teacher can offer valuable suggestions, but as parents you have a responsibility to show an interest in your child's progress. Patience, sincere praise, a show of enthusiasm as your child learns new material, and your occasional participation in music-making sessions at home will be beneficial.

As publishers, it is our pleasure to offer an outstanding course of instruction, prepared for you by three of the world's leading educators. We also recognise that measurable achievement by way of performances and exam grades is a key part of the journey for any burgeoning pianist. In this edition, Alfred's world-famous piano method has been adapted to fulfil the requirements of the standard grades as exemplified by the examination bodies throughout the world.

We sincerely hope your child achieves great success climbing the ladder to musical excellence but more importantly, that they enjoy the journey!

The Publishers

A Note to Teachers

Dear Teachers,

Welcome to Alfred's Basic Graded Piano Course

This Alfred's Basic Graded Piano Course was written in response to many requests from teachers for an Alfred Course that will enable students to pass the graded exams that are so much a part of the learning experience throughout the world. It uses the Lesson book to introduce sight-reading and technique as well as preparation for pieces. It uses the correlated Theory book to prepare for the Theory exam at the same time.

By including some exam pieces from previous practical syllabuses and also a mock theory paper from the theory exam in the correlated theory books, you, as a teacher, can judge perfectly the appropriate time to enter your pupil for the graded exam. This will make passing a formality but more importantly give your pupil the confidence to achieve the merits and distinctions that inspire and reward their hard work.

Here is a basic outline of the Elementary Lesson book:

pgs. 1-3	Introduction to playing
pgs. 4-19	Keyboard orientation; Finger numbering; Essential rhythms; Elementary dynamics; Fluent recognition of key names through letter notes; Melodies in C Position
pgs. 20-26	Introduction of the stave
pgs. 27-51	Slurs and Legato Playing; Intervals in C position (harmonic & melodic)
pgs. 52-55	Staccato playing; G position; Sharps and flats; Introduction to sight-reading
pgs. 56–78	Middle C Position; Tempo markings; Quavers; 2-4; Rests

As you leaf through these books you will notice the clean and uncluttered page design and clear engraving, with attractive art work designed to complement the music and appeal to all.

The authors hope that these pages will help you open the door of the WONDERFUL WORLD OF MUSIC to many students,

Willard A. Palmer, Morton Manus & Amanda Vick Lethco

How to Sit at the Piano

SIT TALL!

Lean slightly forward.

Let arms hang loosely from shoulders.

Elbows slightly higher than keys.

Bench must face piano squarely.

Knees slightly under keyboard.

Feet flat on floor.
Right foot may be slightly forward.

You may place a book or stool under your feet
if they do not reach the floor!

Fingers Have Numbers

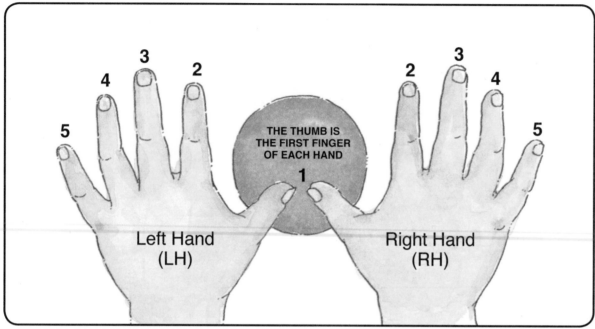

1. Your teacher will draw an outline of your hands on the inside cover of this book.

2. Number each finger of the outline.

3. Hold up both hands with wrists floppy.

- Wiggle both 1's.

- Wiggle both 2's.

- Wiggle both 3's.

- Wiggle both 4's.

- Wiggle both 5's.

Your teacher will call out some fingers for you to wiggle.

Piano Tones

When you play a key, a hammer inside your piano strikes a string to make a tone.

When you drop into the key with a LITTLE weight, you make a SOFT tone.

When you use MORE weight, you make a LOUDER tone.

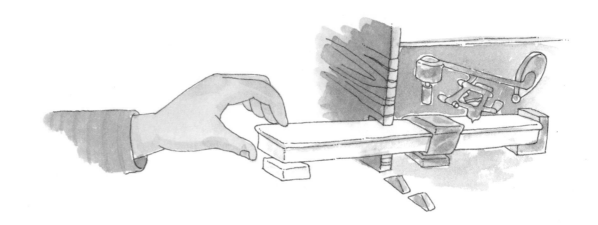

Curve your fingers when you play!

Pretend you have a bubble in your hand.

Hold the bubble gently, so it doesn't break!

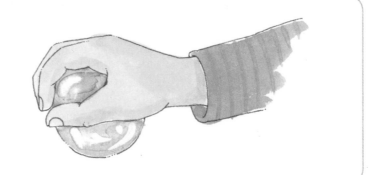

1. Play any white key with the 3rd finger of either hand, softly.
2. See how many times you can repeat the same key, making the tone a little louder each time you play.

Before you play any key you should always decide how soft or loud you want it to sound.

For the first pieces in this book, play with a MODERATELY LOUD tone.

Always LISTEN CAREFULLY to the music you are making!

The Keyboard

The keyboard is made up of white keys and black keys.

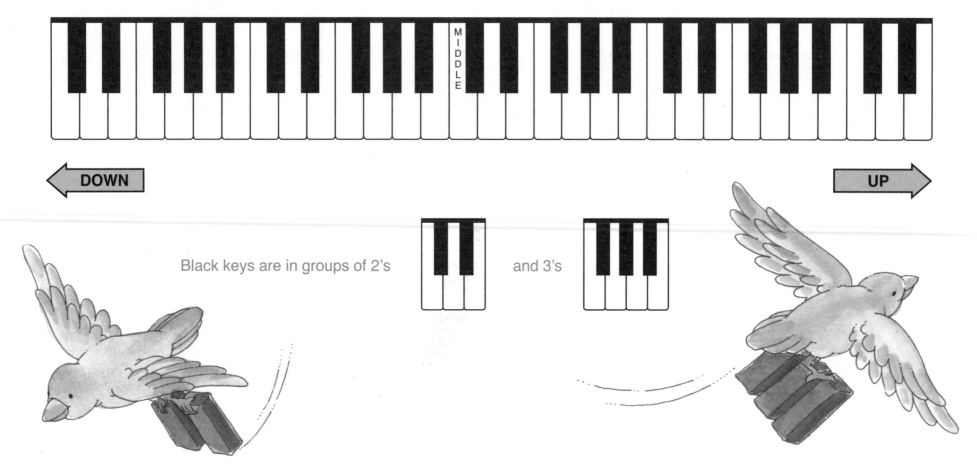

Black keys are in groups of 2's and 3's

1. Using LH 2 3, begin at the middle and play all the 2 black key groups going DOWN the keyboard (both keys at once).

2. Play them again, one key at a time.
   PLAY: LH 2 3.
   SAY: "Step down" as you play each pair.

3. Using RH 2 3, begin at the middle and play all the 2 black key groups going UP the keyboard (both keys at once).

4. Play them again, one key at a time.
   PLAY: RH 2 3.
   SAY: "Step up" as you play each pair.

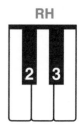

Low Sounds and High Sounds

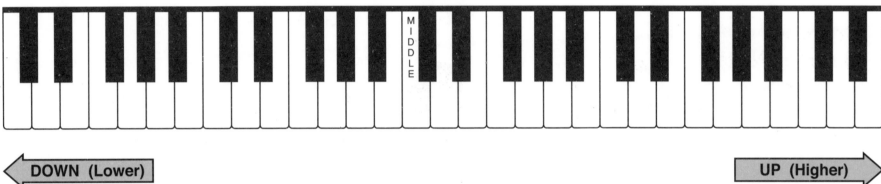

← **DOWN (Lower)**

LOW SOUNDS

UP (Higher) →

HIGH SOUNDS

LH

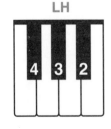

1. Using LH 2 3 4, begin at the middle and play all the 3 black key groups going ← DOWN the keyboard (all 3 keys at once).

2. Play them again, one key at a time.
   PLAY: LH 2 3 4.
   SAY: "Step - ping down."

RH

3. Using RH 2 3 4, begin at the middle and play all the 3 black key groups going UP → the keyboard (all 3 keys at once).

4. Play them again, one key at a time.
   PLAY: RH 2 3 4.
   SAY: "Step - ping up."

Music is made up of **short** notes and **long** notes.
We measure their lengths by **counting.**

Crotchet or Quarter Note
a **short** note.

COUNT: "One"

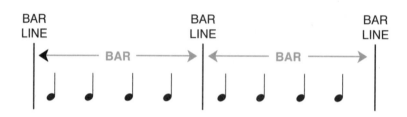

When we clap or tap **ONCE** for each note,
we call it clapping or tapping the **RHYTHM.**
Clap or tap the following rhythm, counting aloud.

BAR LINES divide the music into equal **BARS.**

BAR LINE | ←——— **BAR** ———→ | BAR LINE | ←——— **BAR** ———→ | BAR LINE

Right & Left

1. Play & say the finger numbers.
2. Play & sing the words.

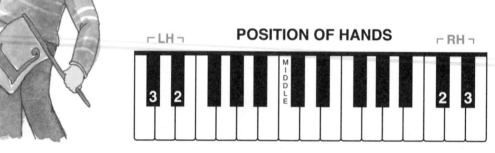

POSITION OF HANDS

⌐ LH ⌐   ⌐ RH ⌐

3 2 ... MIDDLE ... 2 3

RH Fingers:
(Stems UP)

2 3 2 3 | 2 3 2 3

Right hand play - ing, Hear the high notes!

DOUBLE BAR
used at
the end.

LH Fingers:
(Stems DOWN)

2 3 2 3 | 2 3 2 3

Left hand play - ing, Hear the low notes!

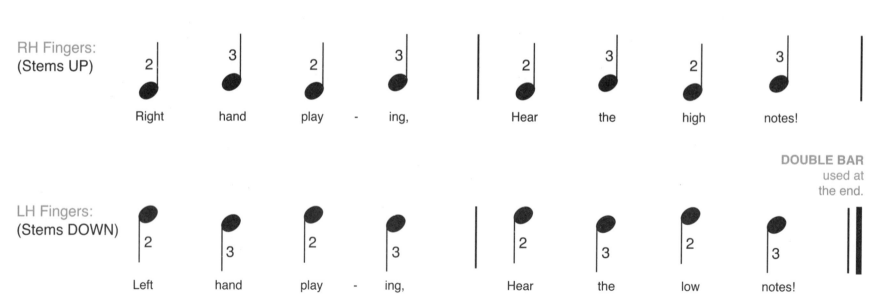

Minim or Half Note

a **long** note.

COUNT: "One - two"

1. Clap (or tap) the following rhythm.
2. Clap **ONCE** for each note, counting aloud as you clap.

Left & Right

1. Clap (or tap) the rhythm, counting aloud.
2. Play & say the finger numbers.
3. Play & sing the words.

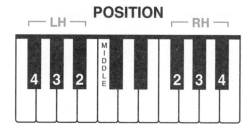

LH Fingers:

2 3 4   4 3 2

Left hand plays;   Sing a - long!

RH Fingers:

2 3 4   4 3 2

Right hand plays;   End of song!

8

1. Clap (or tap) & count.
2. Play & count.
3. Play & sing the words.
4. Play a duet with your teacher.

LEFT HAND POSITION

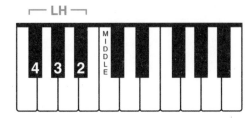

Merrily We Roll Along

(FOR LEFT HAND)

LH Fingers:

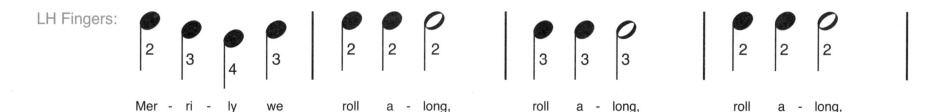

DUET PART: (Student uses black key groups ABOVE the middle of the keyboard.)

THIS PAGE:

NEXT PAGE:

Semibreve or Whole Note

a **very long** note.

o

COUNT: "One - two - three - four"

1. Clap (or tap) the following rhythm.
2. Clap **ONCE** for each note, counting aloud as you clap.

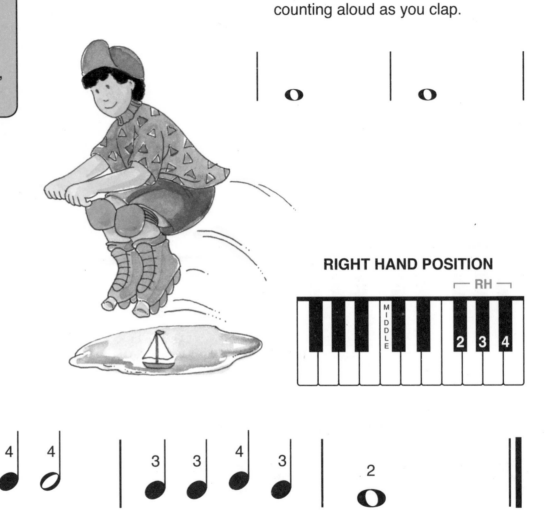

RIGHT HAND POSITION

1. Follow 1–4 at the top of page 8.

O'er the Deep Blue Sea

(FOR RIGHT HAND)

RH Fingers:

| 4 | 3 | 2 | 3 | 4 | 4 | 4 | | 3 | 3 | 4 | 3 | 2 |

Mer - ri - ly we roll a - long,   O'er the deep blue   sea!

2. Play the music on pages 8 & 9 as one song. Count aloud.
3. Play & sing the words.
4. Play a duet with your teacher. Use black key groups **ABOVE** the middle of the keyboard.

Hand-Bells

PART 1 (FOR LEFT HAND)

1. Clap (or tap) & count.
2. Play & count.
3. Play & sing the words.
4. Play a duet with your teacher.

LEFT HAND POSITION

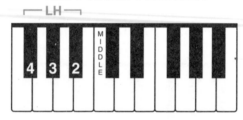

DYNAMIC SIGNS tell us how LOUD or SOFT to play.

p (PIANO) = *SOFT*   *f* (FORTE) = *LOUD*

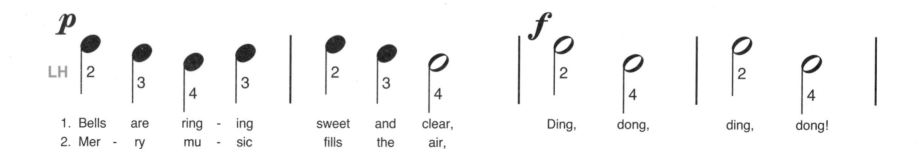

1. Bells   are   ring - ing   sweet   and   clear,

2. Mer - ry   mu - sic   fills   the   air,

Ding,   dong,   ding,   dong!

Hand-Bells

PART 2 (FOR RIGHT HAND)

Follow 1–4 at the top of page 10.
Use these steps for each new piece.

RIGHT HAND POSITION

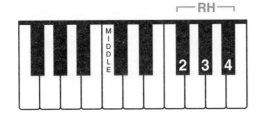

TWO DOTS
mean go back to
the beginning and
play again.

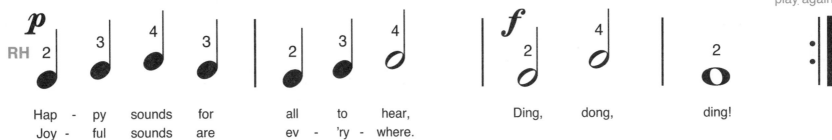

Hap - py sounds for all to hear,
Joy - ful sounds are ev - 'ry - where.

Ding, dong, ding!

DUET PART:

8va throughout

Jolly Old Saint Nicholas

PART 1 (FOR BLACK KEY GROUPS BELOW MIDDLE)

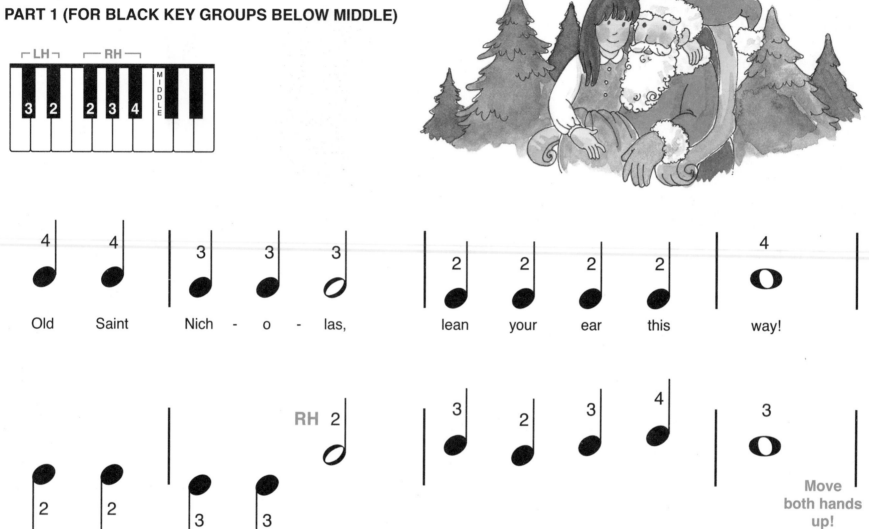

Old Saint Nich - o - las, lean your ear this way!

RH

Move both hands up!

DUET PART: (Student plays on black-key groups ABOVE the middle of the keyboard.)

Jolly Old Saint Nicholas

PART 2 (FOR BLACK KEY GROUPS ABOVE MIDDLE)

After you learn PART 2:

1. Play PART 1 and then PART 2 to make one song!
2. Move both hands to the next higher black key groups and play a duet with your teacher.

Dyno, My Pet Dinosaur

1. Clap (or tap) & count.
2. Play & count.
3. Play & say note names.
4. Play & sing the words.

Follow these steps for each new piece.

RH = Notes with stems UP
LH = Notes with stems DOWN

The C nearest the middle of the keyboard (under the brand name of the piano) is called "Middle C."

MIDDLE C POSITION

LH = 3 2 ① 2 3 = RH

THUMBS on MIDDLE C

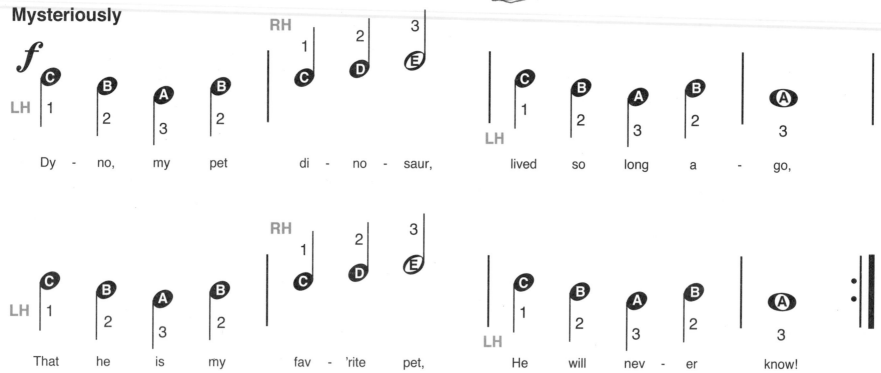

Mysteriously

𝆑

Dy - no,   my   pet   di - no - saur,   lived   so   long   a - go,

That   he   is   my   fav - 'rite   pet,   He   will   nev - er   know!

SUGGESTION: When repeating, you may move the hands to a lower position (with thumbs on a lower C),
if you wish. This will sound more like a dinosaur.

The Zoo

New Dynamic Sign

mf (MEZZO FORTE) = *MODERATELY LOUD*

MIDDLE C POSITION

LH = 5 4 3 2 ① 2 3 4 5 = RH

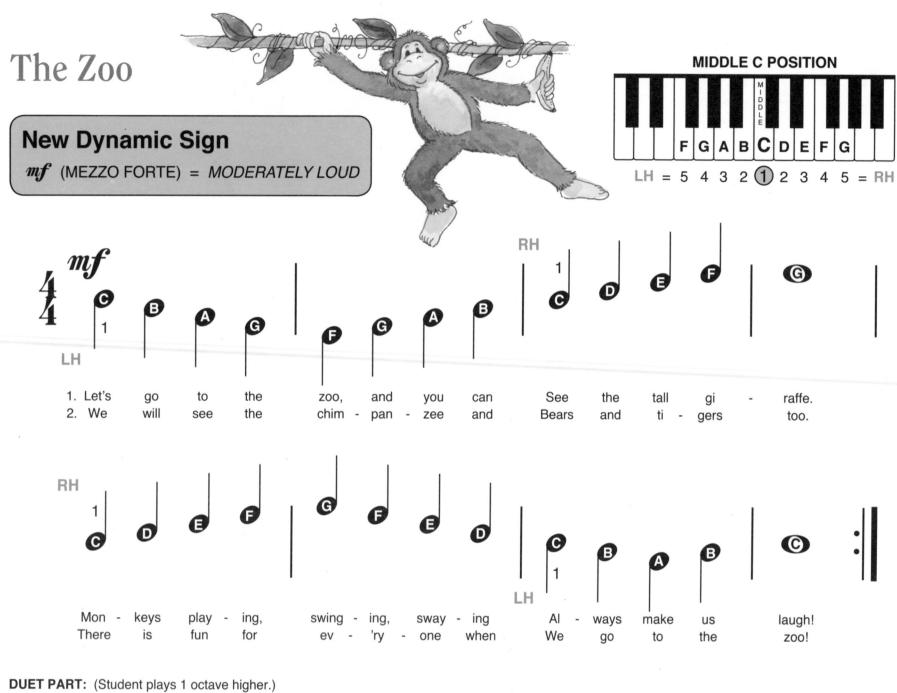

1. Let's go to the zoo, and you can See the tall gi - raffe.
2. We will see the chim - pan - zee and Bears and ti - gers too.

Mon - keys play - ing, swing - ing, sway - ing Al - ways make us laugh!
There is fun for ev - 'ry - one when We go to the zoo!

DUET PART: (Student plays 1 octave higher.)

Playing in a New Position

C POSITION

Dotted Minim or
Dotted Half Note
a **longer** note.

COUNT: "1 - 2 - 3"

1. Clap (or tap) the following rhythm.
2. Clap **ONCE** for each note,
   counting aloud as you clap.

C POSITION

Sailing

mf

RH

1. Come,   come,   come   to   the   sea!
2. Sea   gulls   'round   us   will   play.

Come,   come,   sail - ing   with   me!
We'll   go   sail - ing   a   -   way!

DUET PART: (Student plays 1 octave higher.)

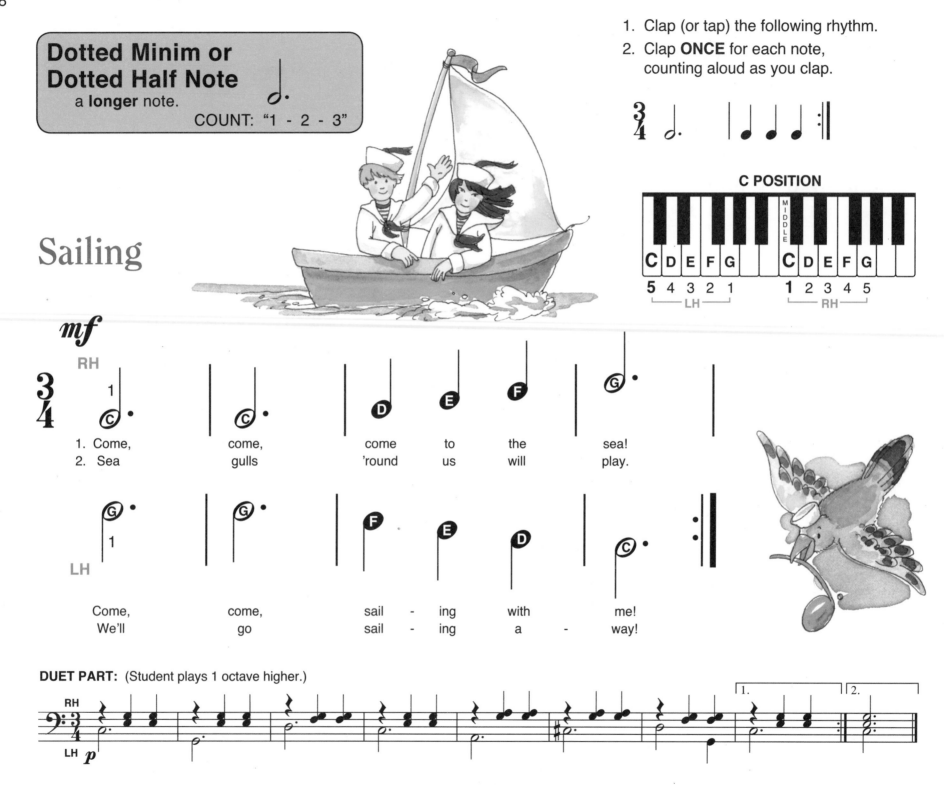

What Can I Share?

C POSITION (same as page 18)

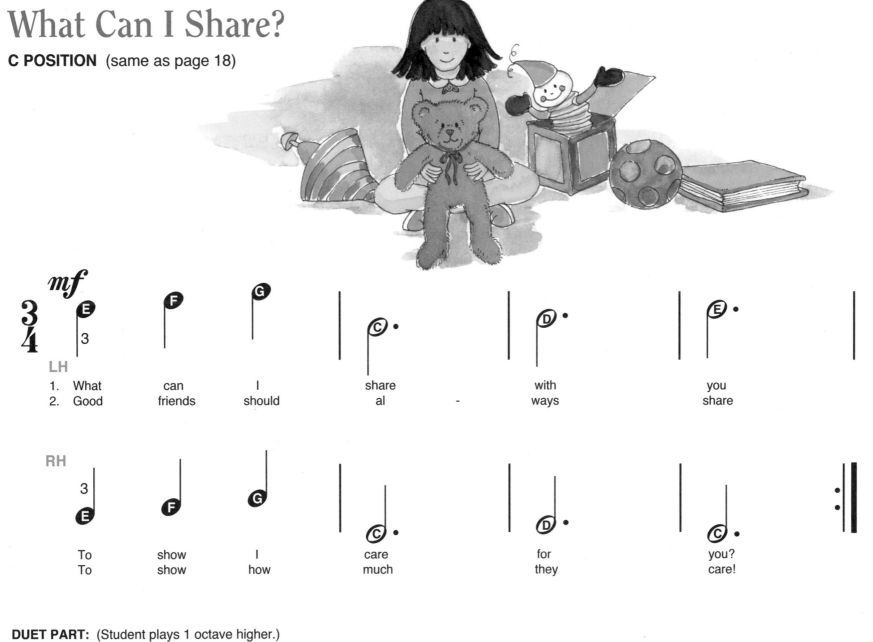

mf

3/4

LH

1. What   can   I   share   with   you
2. Good   friends   should   al - ways   you   share

E(3) F G C D E

RH

E(3) F G C D C

To   show   I   care   for   you?
To   show   how   much   they   care!

DUET PART: (Student plays 1 octave higher.)

The Stave

Music is written on a STAVE of 5 lines and 4 spaces:

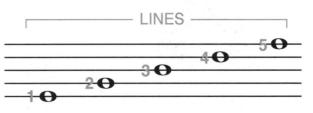

Some notes are written on LINES

Some notes are written in SPACES:

The Bass Stave

The BASS STAVE is indicated by the BASS CLEF sign:

Locates the **F** below the middle of the keyboard.

This sign came from the letter **F:**

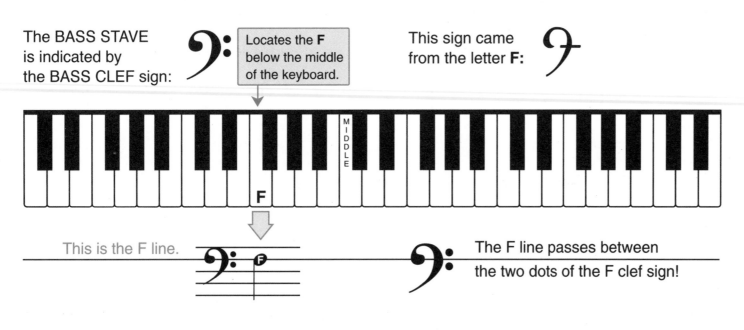

This is the F line.

The F line passes between the two dots of the F clef sign!

By moving up or down from this F, you can name any note on the bass stave.

Notes REPEATED on **same** line or space: REPEAT **same** key.

Notes stepping DOWN to next space or line: step DOWN to next white key.

Notes stepping UP to next space or line: step UP to next white key.

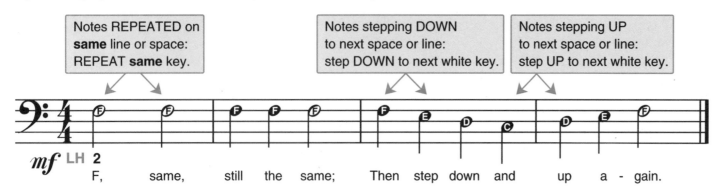

mf LH **2**

F,　　same,　　still　the　same;　　Then　step　down　and　　up　a - gain.

Rain, Rain!

LH C POSITION

Notes ABOVE or ON the middle line have stems pointing DOWN.

Notes BELOW the middle line have stems pointing UP.

LH 5 4 3 2 1

mf

LH 2

Rain, rain, go a - way! Come a - gain an - oth - er day!

Rain, rain, go a - way! My friend _____ wants to play!

(add name)

DUET PART:

p

The Treble Clef Sign

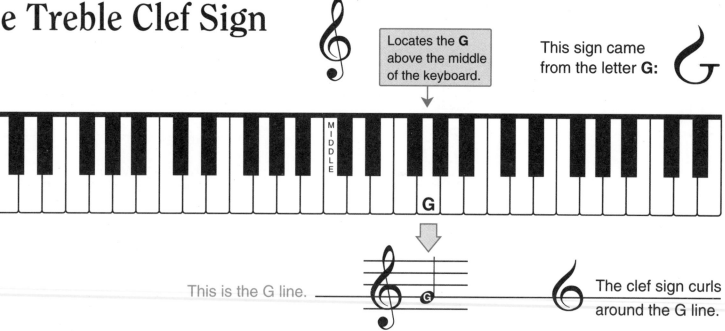

Locates the **G** above the middle of the keyboard.

This sign came from the letter **G:**

This is the G line.

The clef sign curls around the G line.

By moving up or down from this **G,** you can name any note on the treble stave.

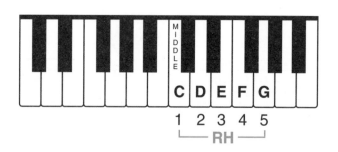

C D E F G
1 2 3 4 5
└─ RH ─┘

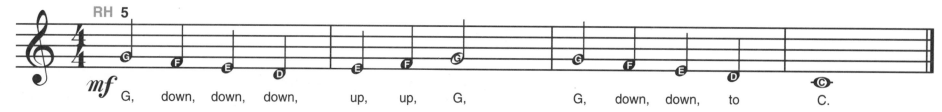

RH 5

mf G, down, down, down, up, up, G, G, down, down, to C.

Gee, We're Glad!

REMEMBER:

The clef sign curls around the **G** line.

RH C POSITION

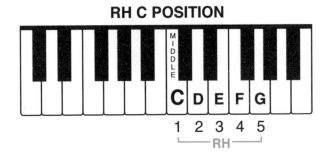

RH **5**

mf Gee, we're glad you came to see us! Come back an - y time you can.

5

Gee, we love to have you vis - it! Please come back a - gain.

DUET PART:

RH

LH *p*

sempre staccato

A Happy Song

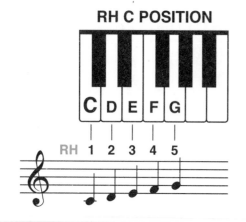

RH C POSITION

f Here's a ver - y hap - py song! Play and sing a - long!

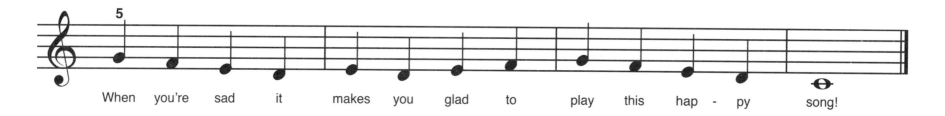

When you're sad it makes you glad to play this hap - py song!

DUET PART:

mf   simile

The Grand Stave

The BASS STAVE and TREBLE STAVE together make the GRAND STAVE.

A short line is used between them for MIDDLE C.

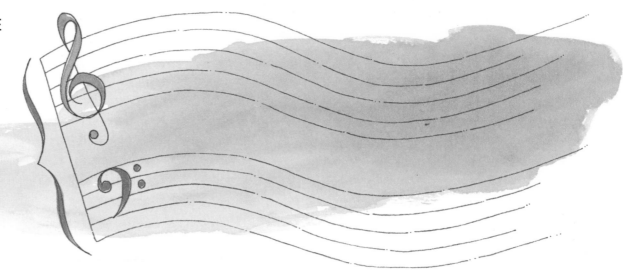

The TREBLE and BASS staves are joined together with a BRACKET:

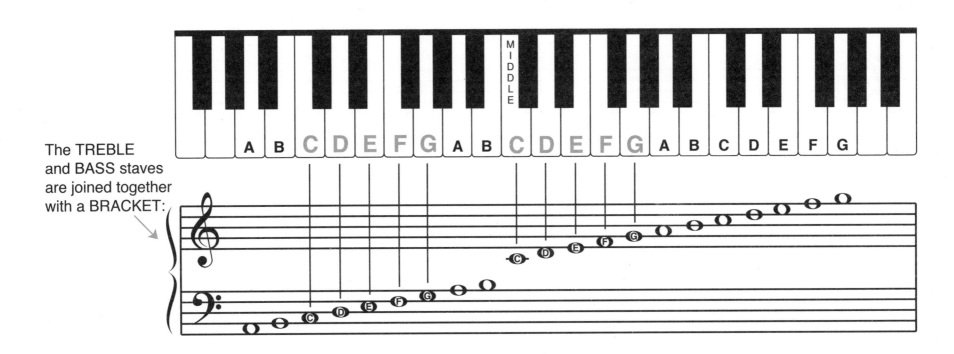

IMPORTANT! Only LH & RH C D E F G need be learned now!

C Position on the Grand Stave

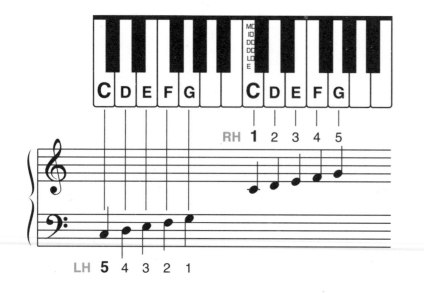

FOR THE REST OF THIS BOOK:

Notes in the TREBLE STAVE 𝄞 will be played with RH.

Notes in the BASS STAVE 𝄢 will be played with LH.

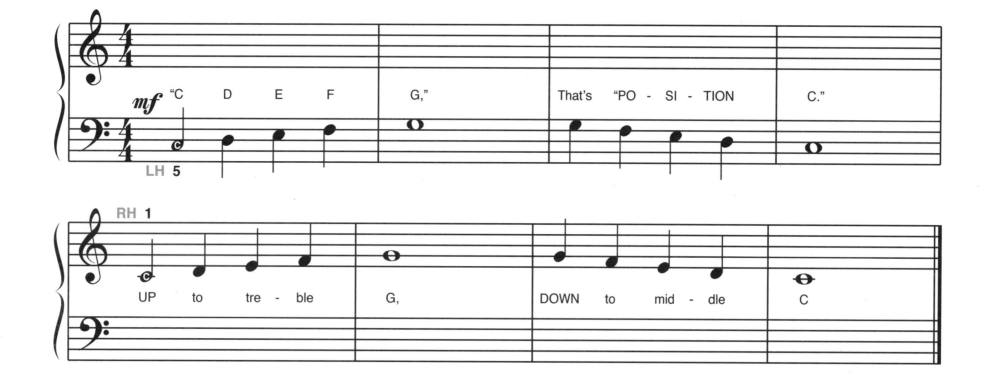

mf "C   D   E   F   G,"   That's   "PO – SI – TION   C."

LH 5

RH 1

UP   to   tre – ble   G,   DOWN   to   mid – dle   C

Legato Playing

Legato means SMOOTHLY CONNECTED.

To play LEGATO correctly, one finger must come up just as another goes down, like the ENDS OF A SEE-SAW.

This piece will make it easy for you to learn to play LEGATO.

PLAY SLOWLY! CONNECT SMOOTHLY! LISTEN CAREFULLY!

SLUR

SLURS mean play LEGATO.

Slurs often divide the music into PHRASES.

A PHRASE is a musical thought or sentence.

See-Saws

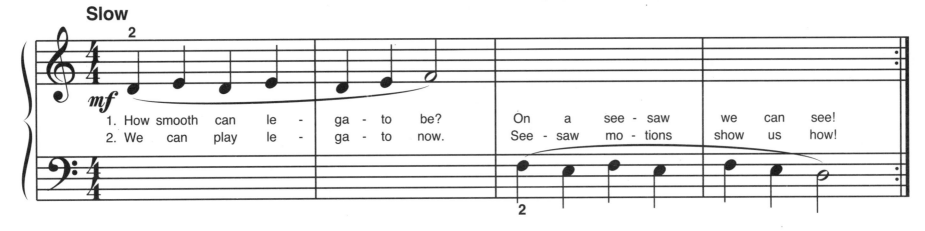

Slow

mf

1. How smooth can le - ga - to be? On a see - saw we can see!
2. We can play le - ga - to now. See - saw mo - tions show us how!

DUET PART: (Student plays 1 octave higher.)

RH

LH *p*

Measuring Distances in Music

Distances from one note to another are measured in INTERVALS, called 2nds, 3rds, etc.

The distance from any white key to the next white key, up or down, is called a **2nd.**

2nds are written LINE-SPACE or SPACE-LINE.

Play, saying "UP a 2nd," etc.

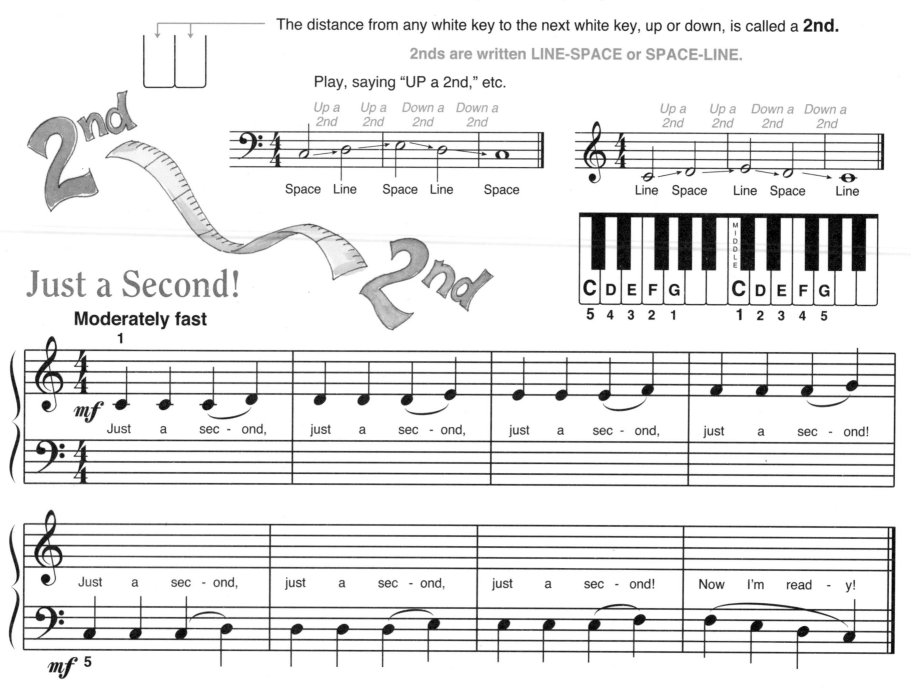

Just a Second!

Moderately fast

mf

Just a sec - ond, just a sec - ond, just a sec - ond, just a sec - ond!

Just a sec - ond, just a sec - ond, just a sec - ond! Now I'm read - y!

mf

Balloons

TIED NOTES
When notes on the SAME LINE or SPACE are joined by a curved line, we call them TIED NOTES. The key is held down for the COMBINED VALUES OF BOTH NOTES.

COUNT: "1 - 2 - 3,   1 - 2 - 3"

Moderately slow

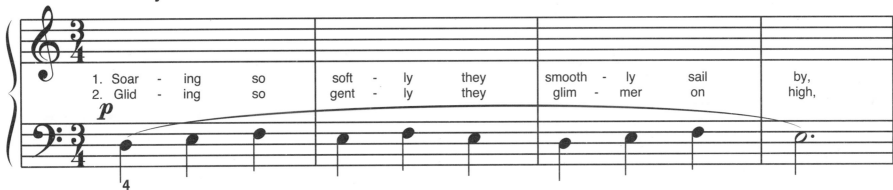

1. Soar - ing so soft - ly they smooth - ly sail by,
2. Glid - ing so gent - ly they glim - mer on high,

(TIED NOTES)

Float - ing like clouds as they fly.
Bright - 'ning like the blue as sum - mer sky.

DUET PART: (Student plays 1 octave higher.)

Calendar Song

When you learn this song you will know
the number of days in each month!

Moderately

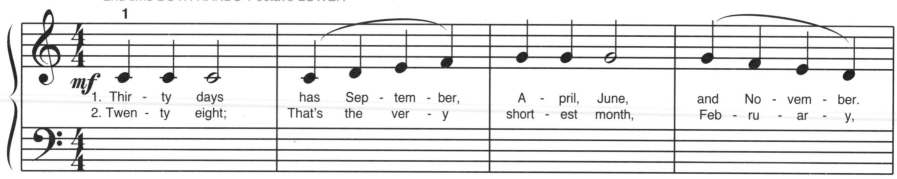

2nd time BOTH HANDS 1 octave LOWER

1. Thir - ty days has Sep - tem - ber, A - pril, June, and No - vem - ber.
2. Twen - ty eight; That's the ver - y short - est month, Feb - ru - ar - y,

All the rest have thir - ty one; Feb - ru - ar - y stands a - lone.
And you add have just one day more *mf* When the year di - vides by four.

DUET PART:

1st time 8va; 2nd time as written

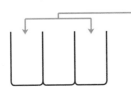

When you skip a white key, the interval is a **3rd.**

3rds are written LINE-LINE or SPACE-SPACE.

Play, saying "UP a 3rd," etc.

Play a Third

Moderately fast

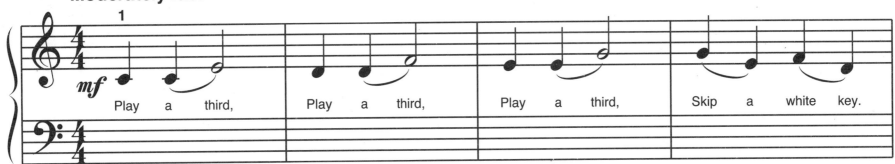

Play a third, Play a third, Play a third, Skip a white key.

Here's a third, Here's a third, Here's a third, I'm sure you know!

Puppies and Guppies

Moderately fast

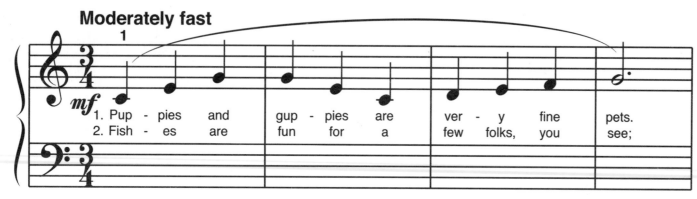

1. Pup - pies and gup - pies are ver - y fine pets.
2. Fish - es are fun for a few folks, you see;

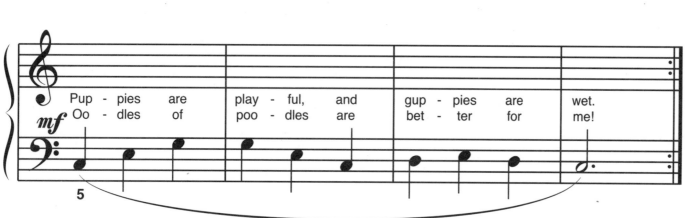

Pup - pies are play - ful, and gup - pies are wet.
Oo - dles of poo - dles and are bet - ter for me!

DUET PART: (Student play 1 octave higher.)

RH

LH *mp*

sempre staccato

Just for Fun!

Moderately fast

2nd time BOTH HANDS 1 octave HIGHER

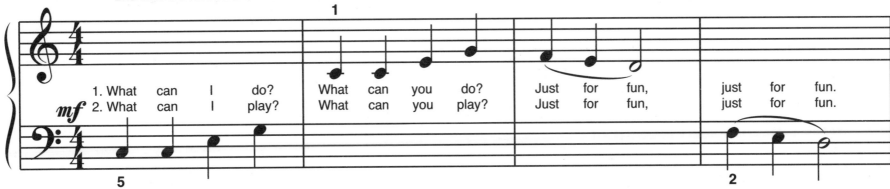

1. What can I do? What can you do? Just for fun, just for fun.
2. What can I play? What can you play? Just for fun, just for fun.

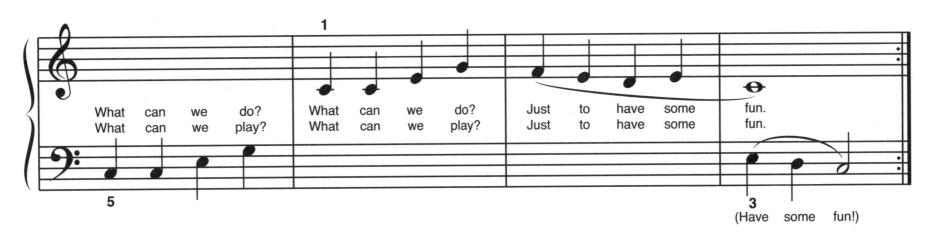

What can we do? What can we do? Just to have some fun.
What can we play? What can we play? Just to have some fun.
(Have some fun!)

DUET PART: (Student plays 1 octave higher.)

More About Intervals

When notes are played separately they make a MELODY.

We call the intervals between melody notes MELODIC INTERVALS.

1. Play these MELODIC 2nds & 3rds. Listen to the sound of each interval.

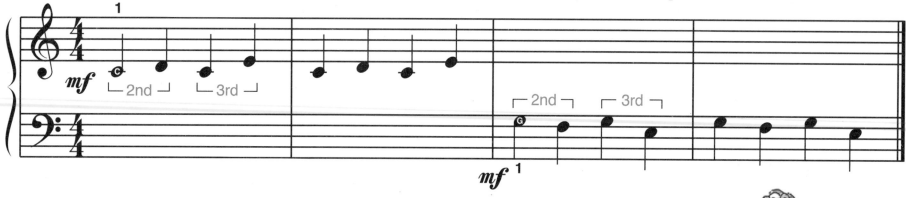

When notes are played together they make HARMONY.

We call the intervals between these notes HARMONIC INTERVALS.

2. Play these HARMONIC 2nds & 3rds. Listen to the sound of each interval.

RESTS are signs of **SILENCE**.

This is a **CROTCHET OR QUARTER REST.**

It means REST FOR THE VALUE of a CROTCHET.

1. Clap (or tap) the following rhythm.
2. Clap **ONCE** for each note, counting aloud.
3. Do not clap for the REST!

Rock Song

Brightly

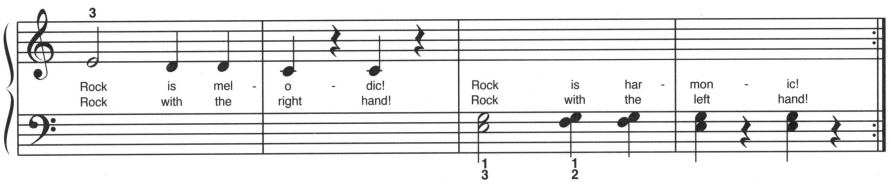

DUET PART (Student plays 1 octave higher.)

36

36

In *ROCKETS,* harmonic intervals (2nds & 3rds) are played by the left hand in the last two bars of each line.

Play the harmonic intervals softer than the melody.
The melody must always be clearly heard!

Rockets

Moderately fast

Rock - ets go up, and they land on the moon!

Rock - ets will trav - el to oth - er worlds soon!

IMPORTANT! Play *ROCKETS* again, playing the 2nd line one octave (8 notes) higher.
The rests at the end of the 1st line give you time to move your hands to the new position!

In this piece, harmonic intervals are played by the right hand in the last two bars of each line.

Play the harmonic intervals softer than the melody, so the melody can always be clearly heard!

Sea Divers

Moderately slow

Down in the o - cean the sea div - ers go.

May - be they'll find man - y treas - ures be - low!

IMPORTANT! Play *SEA DIVERS* again, playing the 2nd line one octave lower!

38

When you skip 2 white keys, the interval is a **4th.**

4ths are written LINE-SPACE or SPACE-LINE.

Play, saying "UP a 4th," etc.

Play a Fourth

Moderately fast

Play a fourth and then a third. That's the best I ev - er heard!

Play them with the oth - er hand. You're the great - est in the land!

DUET PART (Student plays 1 octave higher.)

Old Uncle Bill

Before playing hands together:

1. Play the left hand. Name each harmonic interval.

2. Play the right hand. Name each melodic interval.

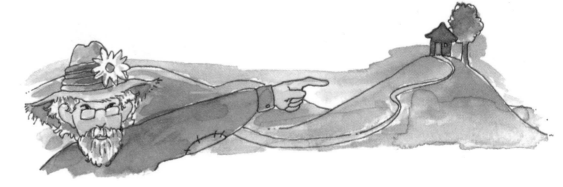

f-*p* means
1st time *f*,
2nd time *p*.

Moderately fast

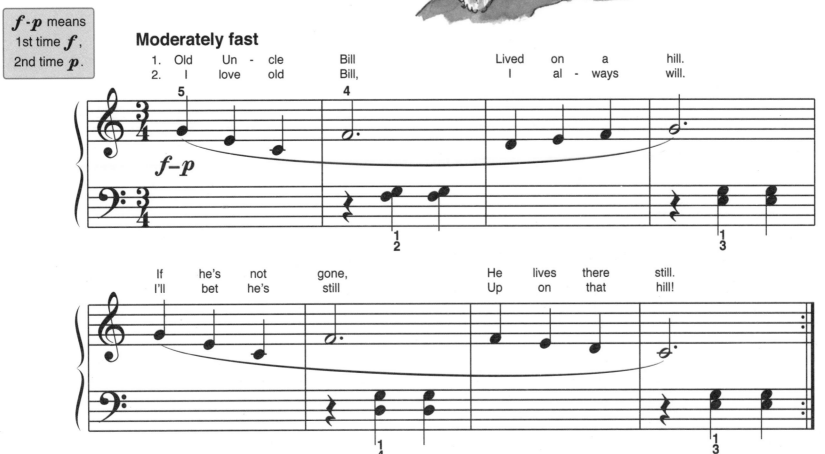

1. Old Un - cle Bill Lived on a hill.
2. I love old Bill, I al - ways will.

If he's not gone, He lives there still.
I'll bet he's still Up on that hill!

DUET PART (Student plays 1 octave higher.)

Love Somebody

Before playing hands together:

1. Play the left hand. Name each harmonic interval.
2. Play the right hand. Name each melodic interval.

> This is a **SEMIBREVE OR WHOLE REST.**
>
> It means REST FOR THE VALUE of a SEMIBREVE or any WHOLE BAR.

Merrily

1. Love some - bod - y, yes I do! Love some - bod - y, won't say who!
2. Love some - bod - y; want to hear? Let me whis - per in your ear.

Love some - bod - y, can you guess Who's the one that I love best?
Love some - bod - y, now you've guessed! You're the one that I love best!

f both times

DUET PART (Student plays 1 octave higher.)

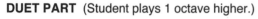

8va throughout

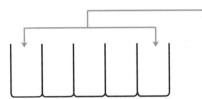

When you skip 3 white keys, the interval is a **5th.**

5ths are written LINE-LINE or SPACE-SPACE.

Play, saying "UP a 5th," etc.

My Fifth

Seriously

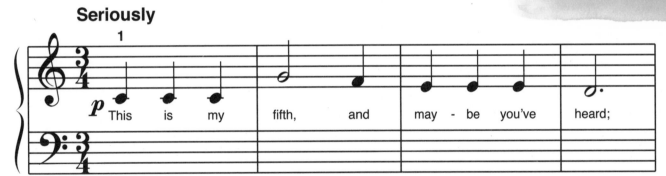

This is my fifth, and may - be you've heard;

Ludwig van Beethoven

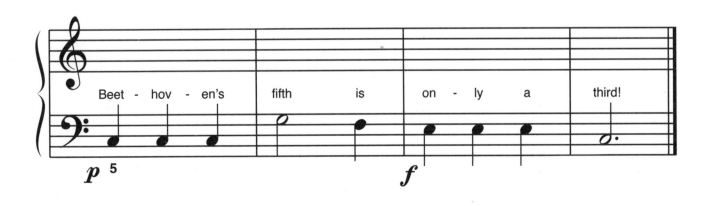

Beet - hov - en's fifth is on - ly a third!

The Donkey

Before playing hands together, play LH alone, naming each harmonic interval.

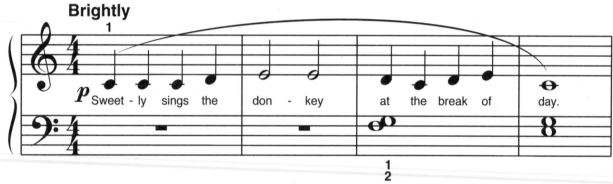

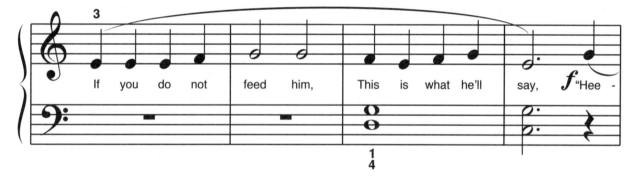

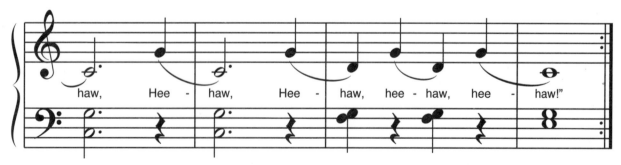

TEACHER'S NOTE: *THE DONKEY* may be played as a ROUND for 2 or 3 pianos. The 2nd piano begins after the 1st has played 4 bars. The 3rd piano begins after the 2nd has played 4 bars. Play 4 times.

Playing in G Position

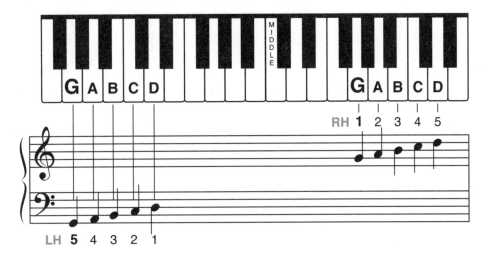

Play & say the note names.

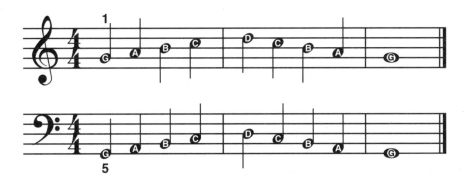

Position G

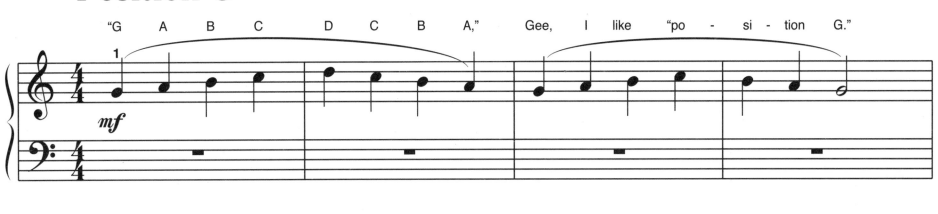

"G A B C D C B A," Gee, I like "po - si - tion G."

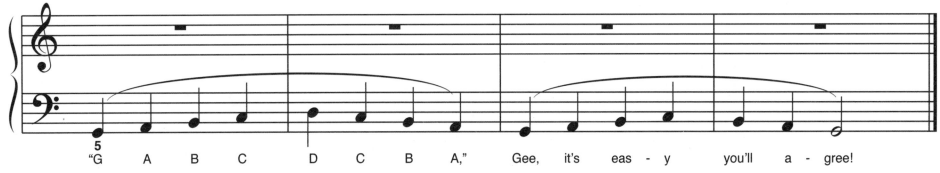

"G A B C D C B A," Gee, it's eas - y you'll a - gree!

Willie & Tillie

(A RIDDLE)

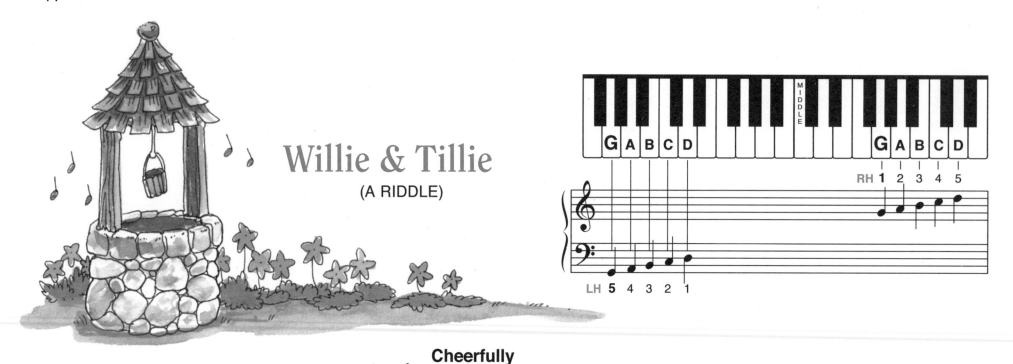

INCOMPLETE BAR

Some pieces begin with an INCOMPLETE BAR. The first bar in this piece has only **1** beat. The **2** missing beats are found in the last bar!

Cheerfully

mf

1. My old Un cle Wil lie loves dear old Aunt Til lie; He
2. They're both fond of fid dles and puz zles and rid dles, But

And
Now

al - so likes bass - es and dou - ble bas - soons.
they nev - er cared much for games or for rhymes.

For the answer, turn the book upside down.

Because of their names, Willie and Tillie decided that they like only things that are spelled with double letters.

Jingle Bells!

G POSITION (See pg. 50)

Merrily

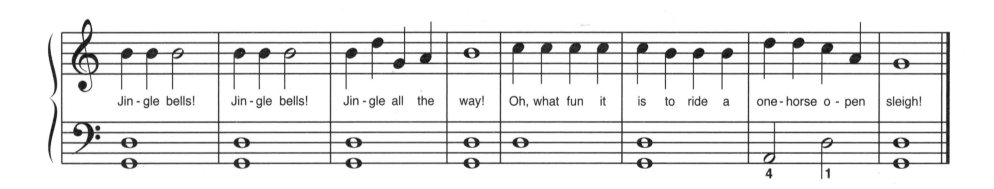

Jin - gle bells! Jin - gle bells! Jin - gle all the way! Oh, what fun it is to ride a one-horse o - pen sleigh!

Jin - gle bells! Jin - gle bells! Jin - gle all the way! Oh, what fun it is to ride a one-horse o - pen sleigh!

DUET PART

8va throughout

legato

A Friend Like You

This piece begins with an incomplete bar of **3** beats. The missing beat is in the last bar.

Before playing hands together, play the LH alone, naming each harmonic interval.

This is a **MINIM** or **HALF REST.**

It means REST FOR THE VALUE of a MINIM.

Moderately slow

1. A friend like you   is hard to find.
2. Where could I find   a friend like you?

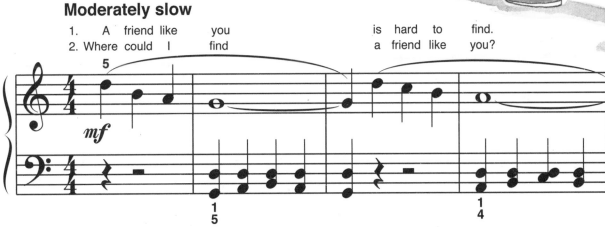

You're al - ways   true,   You're al - ways   kind.
A friend so   kind,   So good, so   true.

The SHARP SIGN before a note means play the next key to the RIGHT, whether BLACK or WHITE.

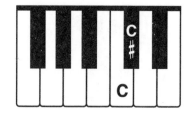

When a sharp (♯) appears before a note, it applies to that note for the rest of the bar.

Circle the notes that are SHARP:

My Robot

Moderately fast

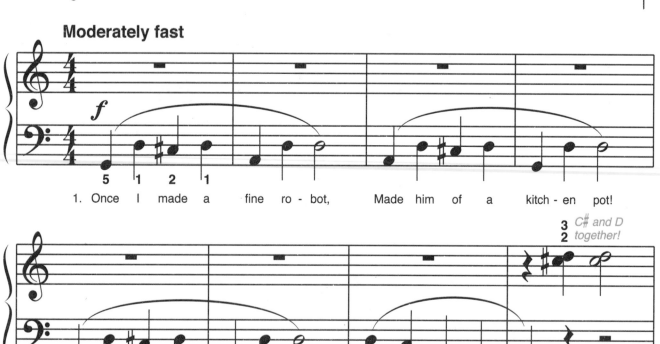

1. Once I made a fine ro - bot, Made him of a kitch - en pot!

When I fin - ished my ro - bot, He said, "Thanks a lot!"

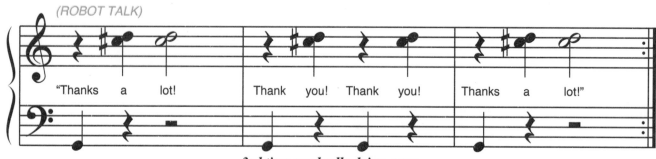

(ROBOT TALK)

"Thanks a lot! Thank you! Thank you! Thanks a lot!"

3rd time gradually dying away - - - - - - - - - - - - - - - - - -

2nd Verse

"Hope you don't think I am rude,
But please bring me something good.
Pots are programmed to hold food.
Bring me all you've got!"
"Thanks a lot!" *etc.*

3rd Verse

If you make a new robot,
Please don't use a kitchen pot.
He'll eat all the food you've got,
And say, "Thanks a lot!"
"Thanks a lot!" *etc.*

The FLAT SIGN
before a note means
play the next key to the LEFT,
whether BLACK or WHITE.

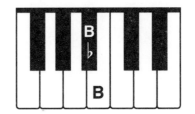

When a flat (♭) appears before a note,
it applies to that note for the rest of the bar.

Circle the notes that are FLAT:

Rockin' Tune

Moderately fast

1. If you're feel - in' blue, if you're feel - in' kind - a wea - ry,
2. Play this Rock - in' Tune, it will sure - ly make you cheer - y;

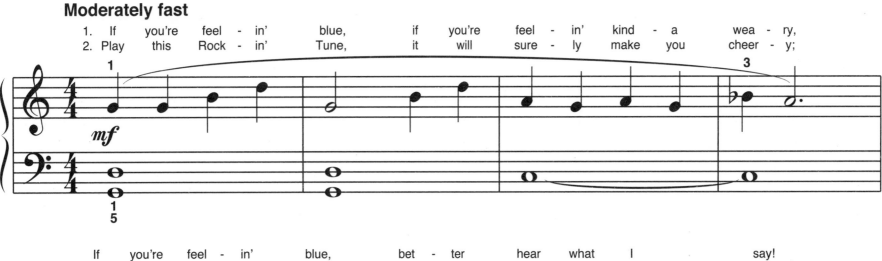

If you're feel - in' blue, bet - ter hear what I say!
When you feel in trou - ble, just rock it a - way!

50

Ancient Song

Moderately, like tom-toms

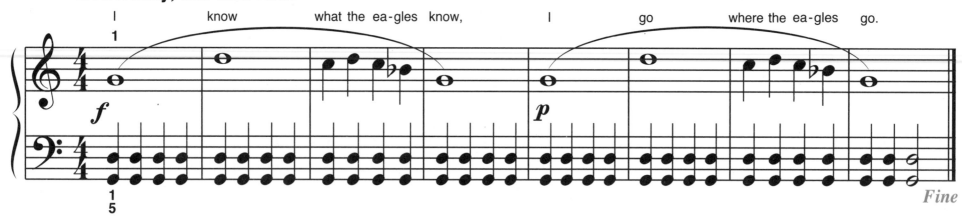

I know what the ea-gles know, I go where the ea-gles go.

f ... *p* ... *Fine*

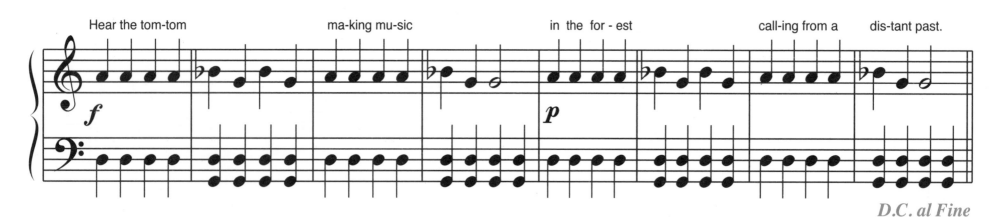

Hear the tom-tom ma-king mu-sic in the for-est call-ing from a dis-tant past.

f ... *p* ... *D.C. al Fine*

D.C. al Fine (Da Capo al Fine) means repeat from the beginning and play to the end *(Fine)*.

Money Can't Buy Ev'rything!

C POSITION REVIEW

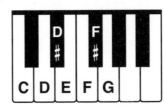

March time

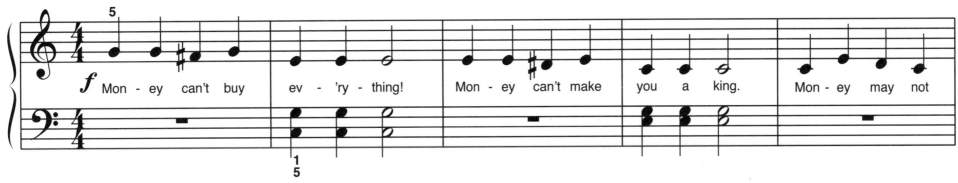

Money can't buy ev-'ry-thing! Mon-ey can't make you a king. Mon-ey may not

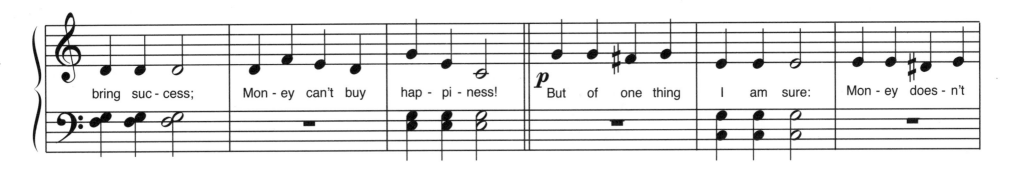

bring suc-cess; Mon-ey can't buy hap-pi-ness! But of one thing I am sure: Mon-ey does-n't

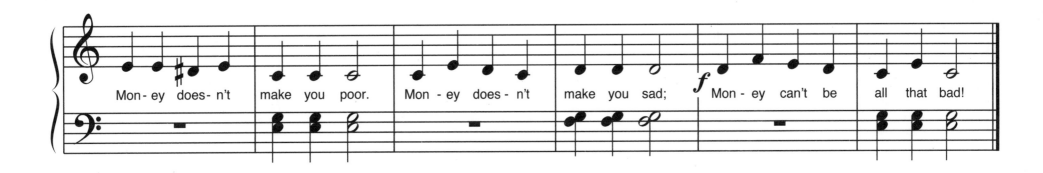

Mon-ey does-n't make you poor. Mon-ey does-n't make you sad; Mon-ey can't be all that bad!

Raindrops (Staccato Playing)

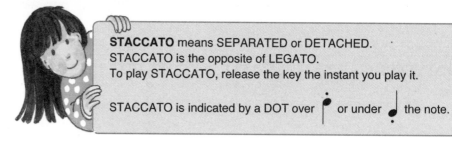

STACCATO means SEPARATED or DETACHED.
STACCATO is the opposite of LEGATO.
To play STACCATO, release the key the instant you play it.

STACCATO is indicated by a DOT over ♩ or under ♩ the note.

Moderately fast

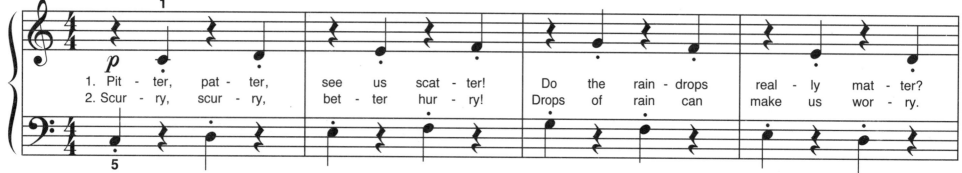

p

1. Pit - ter, pat - ter, see us scat - ter! Do the rain - drops real - ly mat - ter?
2. Scur - ry, scur - ry, bet - ter hur - ry! Drops of rain can make us wor - ry.

Hel - ter skel - ter, run for shel - ter, Just be - cause of drops of rain!
Drip and drop, the game must stop, and just be - cause of drops of rain!

It's Halloween!

NEW DYNAMIC SIGNS

CRESCENDO
(gradually louder)

DIMINUENDO
(gradually softer)

Moderately slow

2nd time play both hands
1 octave (8 notes) lower.

p

1. Gob - lins run - ning down the street, They will get much to eat,
2. Jack - o' - lan - terns, what a sight! You may get quite a fright,

It's the night for "trick or treat," It's Hal - low - een!
When the ghosts come out to - night! It's Hal - low - een!

About Sight-Reading: Rhythm

Sight-reading is a very useful skill that helps us learn pieces very quickly.

To sight-read is to play a piece from sight as if you had already practised it!

To be a successful sight-reader, preparation is very important; here are some useful steps we can take to prepare for each exercise:

1. Look at the time signature and title, and try to imagine the type of piece it might be.
2. Count out the rhythm and try to hear it in your head.
3. Check your hand position and place your hands quietly on the keyboard.
4. Count a bar in your head (or out loud) then begin to play.

54

Oom-Pa-Pa!

This is an **ACCENT SIGN:** >

When there is an ACCENT SIGN over or under a note, play that note LOUDER.

Moderately fast

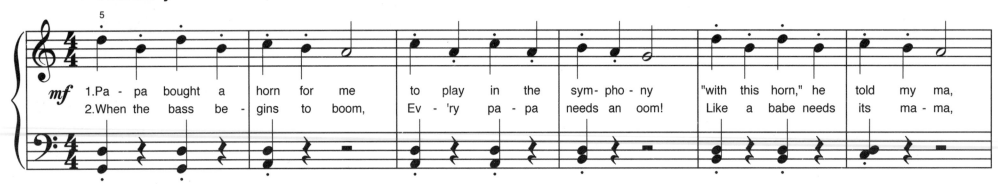

1.Pa - pa bought a horn for me to play in the sym - pho - ny "with this horn," he told my ma,
2.When the bass be - gins to boom, Ev - 'ry pa - pa needs an oom! Like a babe needs its ma - ma,

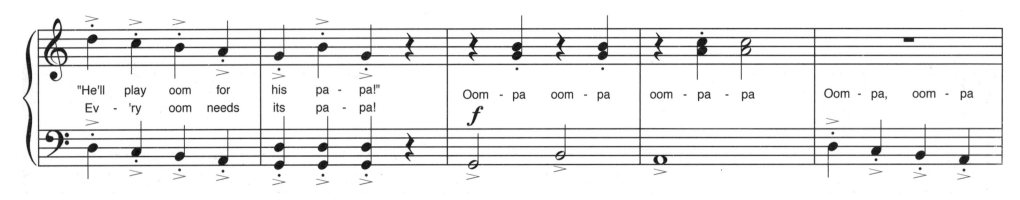

"He'll play oom for his pa - pa!" Oom - pa oom - pa oom - pa - pa Oom - pa, oom - pa
Ev - 'ry oom needs its pa - pa!

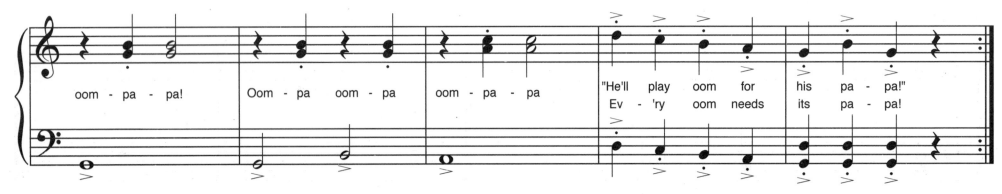

oom - pa - pa! Oom - pa oom - pa oom - pa - pa "He'll play oom for his pa - pa!"
Ev - 'ry oom needs its pa - pa!

The Clown

Moderately Fast

mf

See the fun - ny, fun - ny clown.   He climbs up and he falls down!   You will nev - er see him frown!   He's a fun - ny

clown.   *f* Al - ways be a glad clown!   Al - ways steal the

Fine

show!   *p* When you are a sad clown nev - er let us know.

D.C. al Fine

REMEMBER: *D.C. al Fine* (**Da Capo al Fine**) means *repeat from the beginning and play to the end* (*Fine*).

56

Playing in Middle C Position

LH: Just 3 new notes—A, B, C.
Play and say the note names.

NEW NOTES

RH: Same as C Position.

Thumbs on C

Moderately slow

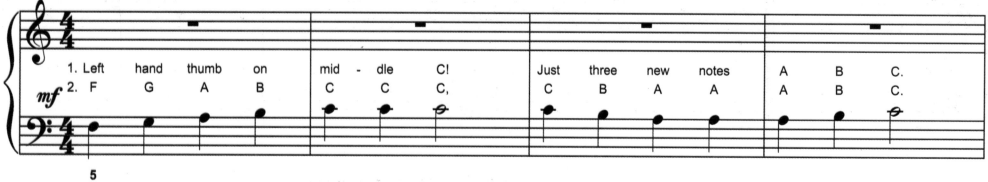

1. Left hand thumb on mid - dle C! Just three new notes A B C.
2. F G A B C C C, C B A A A B C.

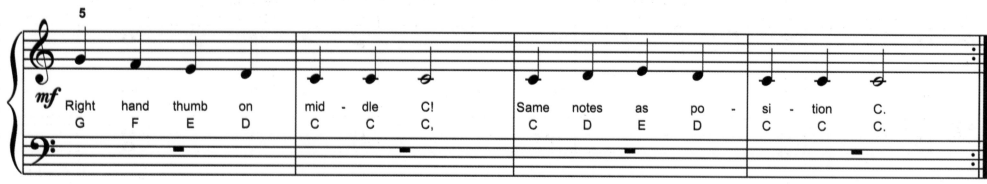

Right hand thumb on mid - dle C! Same notes as po - si - tion C.
G F E D C C C, C D E D C C C.

The Purple Cow

1. In bars 1-8, write the note names in the boxes.
2. Play!

Moderately Fast

Fine

D.C. al Fine

This is the best known poem by Gelett Burgess, who later wrote the following:

Ah yes! I wrote "The Purple Cow,"
I'm sorry now I wrote it.
But I can tell you anyhow,
I'll kill you if you quote it!

Tempo Marks

TEMPO is an Italian word. It means "RATE OF SPEED."

Words indicating how fast or slow to play are called **TEMPO MARKS**.

Here are some of the most important tempo marks:

ALLEGRO = Quickly, happily.   **ANDANTE** = Moving along. The word actually means "walking."

MODERATO = Moderately.   **ADAGIO** = Slowly.

The word **moderato** is sometimes used with one of the other words.

Example: **Allegro moderato** = moderately fast.

Waltz Time

Bring out the LH melody.

SUGGESTION: Repeat with both hands one octave higher.

The Rainbow

This sign is called a **FERMATA.**

Hold the note under the FERMATA longer than its value.

Andante (moving along)

There's red, or-ange yel-low, and green, and blue, and in-di-go, vi-o-let, ev-'ry hue, and

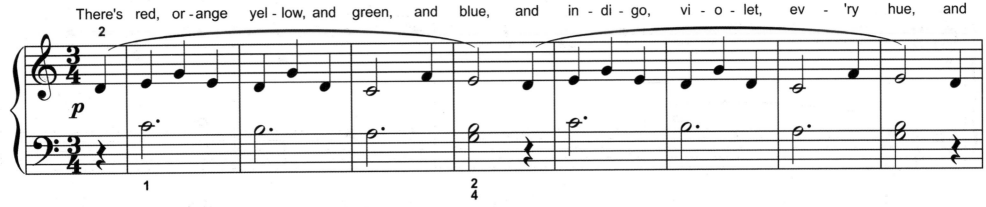

Adagio (slowly)

where can you find a pot of pure gold? At the end of the rain-bow, or so I've been told!

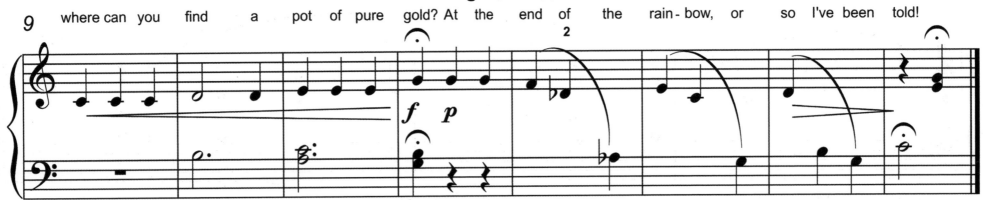

Good Morning to You!

Allegro (quickly, happily)

Good morn - ing to you! Good morn - ing to you! Good

morn - ing, dear   Good morn - ing to you!

Quavers or Eighth Notes

Two quavers are played in the time of **one crotchet.**

When a piece contains quavers,

count: "one-and" or "crotch-et" for each crotchet;

count: "one-and" or "qua-ver" for each pair of quavers.

> **Quavers**
> are usually played
> in **pairs.**
>
> COUNT: **"one-and"**
> or: **"qua-ver"**

Clap (or tap) these notes, counting aloud:

Happy Birthday!

> *HAPPY BIRTHDAY* is exactly the same as *GOOD MORNING TO YOU*, except for the **QUAVERS!**

Allegro

Hap - py   Birth - day   to   you!   Hap - py   Birth - day   to   you!   Hap - py

Birth - day,   Dear   Hap - py   Birth - day   to   you!

62

The Windmill

Andante

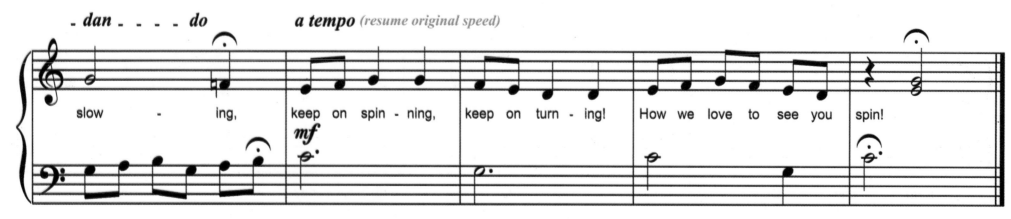

More About Sight-Reading: Melody

This time we are going to add some more steps and skips to our rhythms.

Can you remember the preparation steps?

1. Look at the time signature and title, and try to imagine the type of piece it might be.

2. Count out the rhythm and try to hear it in your head.

3. Look at the melodies and try to sing them in your head: use the letter names if it helps.

4. Check your hand position and place your hands quietly on the keyboard.

5. Count a bar in your head (or out loud) then begin to play.

6. Try to hear the rhythm tapping in your head throughout allowing the notes to play as the music moves forward.

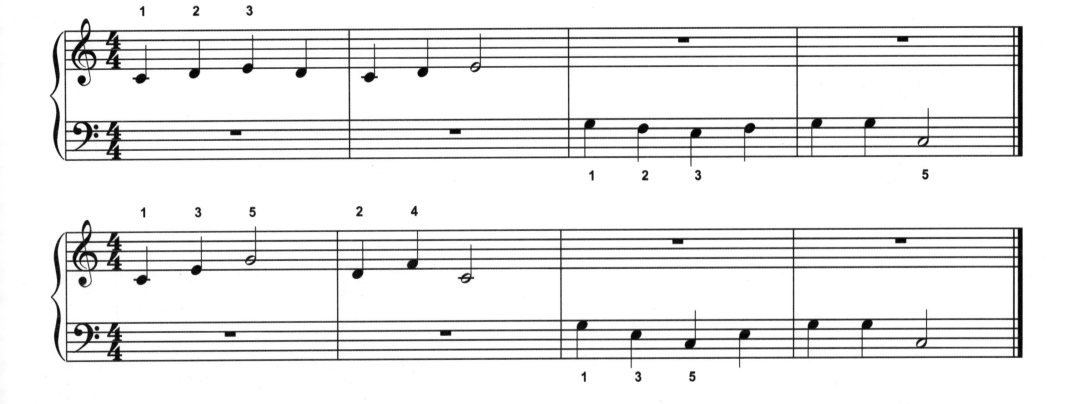

A New Time Signature

2/4 means 2 beats to each bar.

a **crotchet** gets one beat.

Yankee Doodle

A **SEMIBREVE REST** is used to indicate a whole bar of silence in **2/4** time.

Allegro moderato

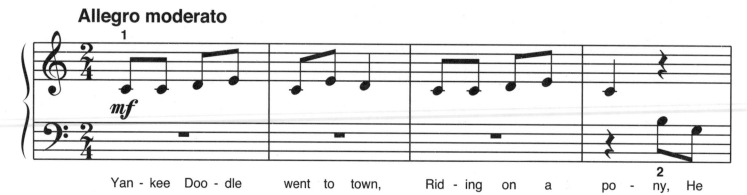

Yan - kee Doo - dle   went to town,   Rid - ing on a   po - ny, He

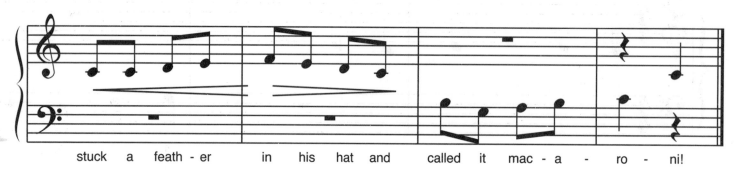

stuck a feath - er   in his hat and   called it mac - a - ro - ni!

DUET PART: (Student plays 1 octave higher.)

G Position   with LH an Octave Higher

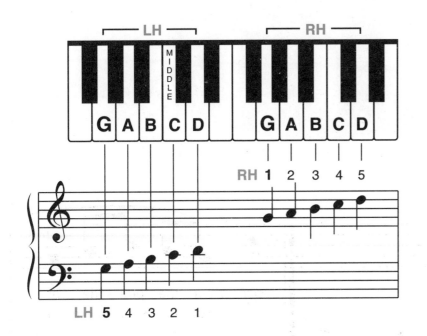

In this NEW G POSITION, the LEFT HAND plays ONE OCTAVE HIGHER than before.

The RIGHT HAND remains in the same position.

There is only ONE new LH note to learn.

New Position G

Moderato

1. G, G, Gee what fun, play-ing up to D! G, the mu - sic sounds so good in new po - si- tion G!
2. G G G A B, B A B C D, G G D D B B G G D C B A G.

A Cowboy's Song

Lazily

p

5 1 4 1 3

mf 1. On the prai - rie at
2. But the stars seem to

night,
say,

On my po - ny I roam
As they guide me a - long.

Ov - er head, stars are
"We will show you the

4

bright;
way;

I'm a long way from home!
We won't let you go wrong!"

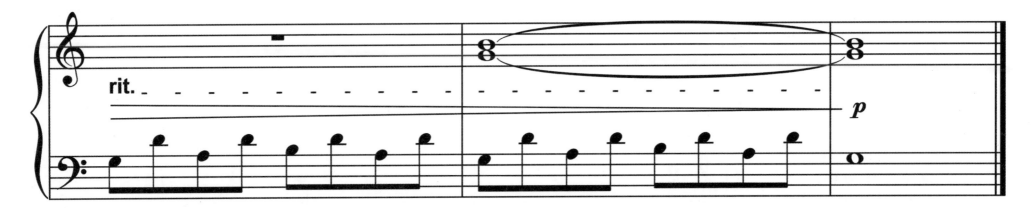

rit.

p

A special WESTERN EFFECT may be produced by playing the pairs of quavers a bit unevenly, in a "lilting" style:

long short long short, *etc.*

SUGGESTION: Try playing *A COWBOY'S SONG* with LH **8va lower**, in the old G position.

The Damper Pedal

The **RIGHT PEDAL** is called the **DAMPER PEDAL**.

When you hold the damper pedal down, any note you sound continues after you release the key.

The **RIGHT FOOT** is used on the damper pedal.

Always keep your heel on the floor; use your ankle like a hinge

This sign shows when the damper pedal is to be used:

This sign means: **PEDAL DOWN**

HOLD PEDAL   **PEDAL UP**

Pedal Play

This easy PEDAL STUDY will show you how the damper pedal causes the tones to continue to sound, EVEN AFTER YOUR HANDS HAVE RELEASED THE KEYS.

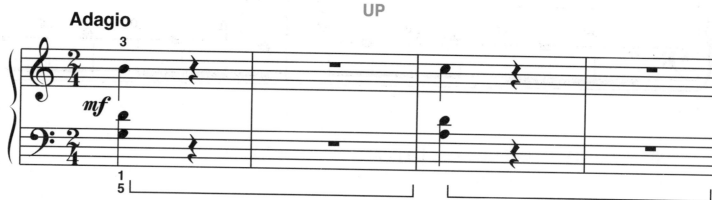

Press the pedal down as you play each group of notes. Hold it down through the rests.

Play **VERY SLOWLY** and **LISTEN.**

Harp Song

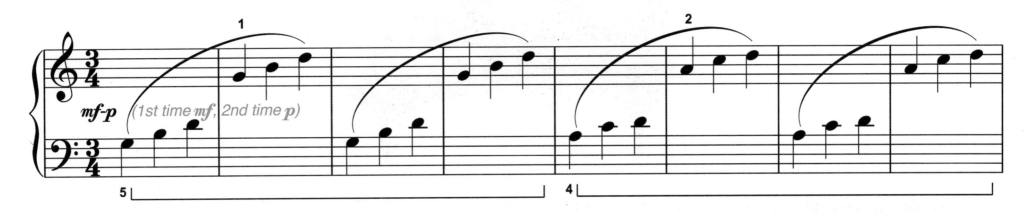

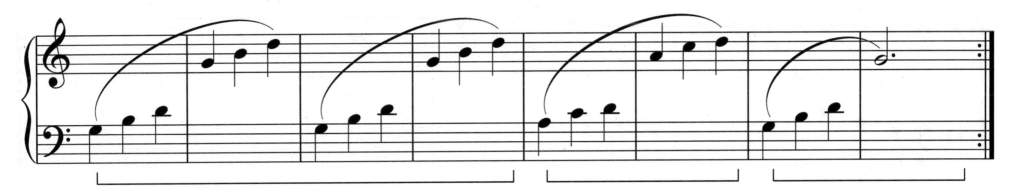

VERY IMPORTANT!

Also play *HARP SONG* in the following ways:

1. Play the 3rd and 4th bars of each four bar phrase one octave higher than written.

2. Play the 1st and 2nd bars of each four bar phrase one octave lower than written.

3. Any combination of the above two ways.

Concert Time

Fine

D.C. al Fine

* **8**va applies only to the STAVE below it unless "both hands" is added.

Music Box Rock

Allegro

Play both hands 8va throughout.

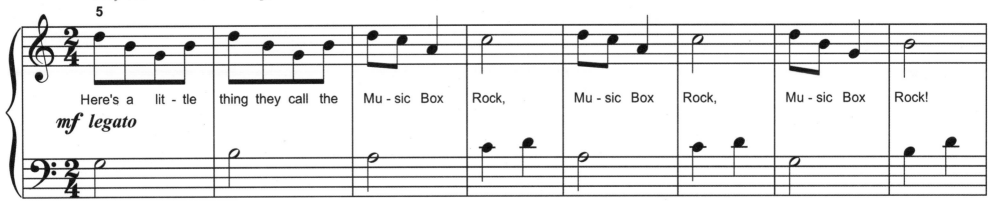

Here's a lit - tle thing they call the Mu - sic Box Rock, Mu - sic Box Rock, Mu - sic Box Rock!

mf **legato**

Repeat as
many times
as you like!

last time ritardando to end _____

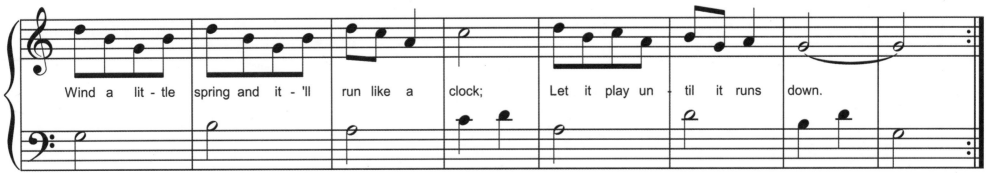

Wind a lit - tle spring and it - 'll run like a clock; Let it play un - til it runs down.

This is a **QUAVER or EIGTH NOTE REST.**

It means REST FOR THE VALUE OF A QUAVER.

When quavers appear singly, they look like this:

Single quavers are often used with quaver rests:

COUNT: "one - and"
OR: "qua - ver"

The Magic Man

Mysteriously

1. Who can pull a rab - bit out of
2. Who can van - ish an - y - thing and

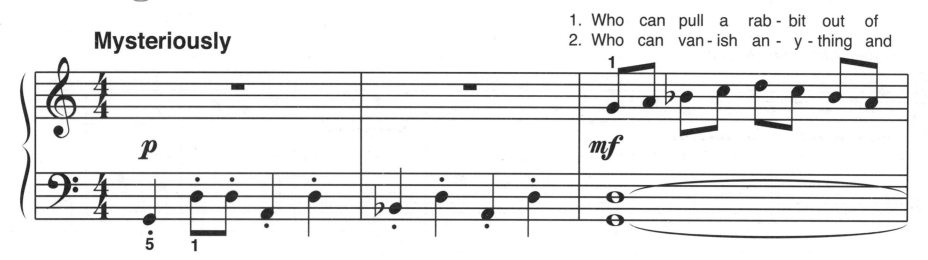

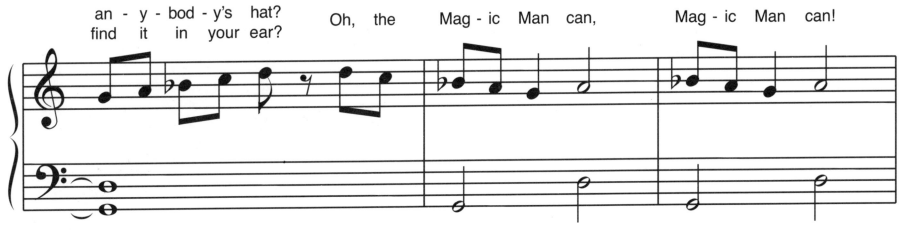

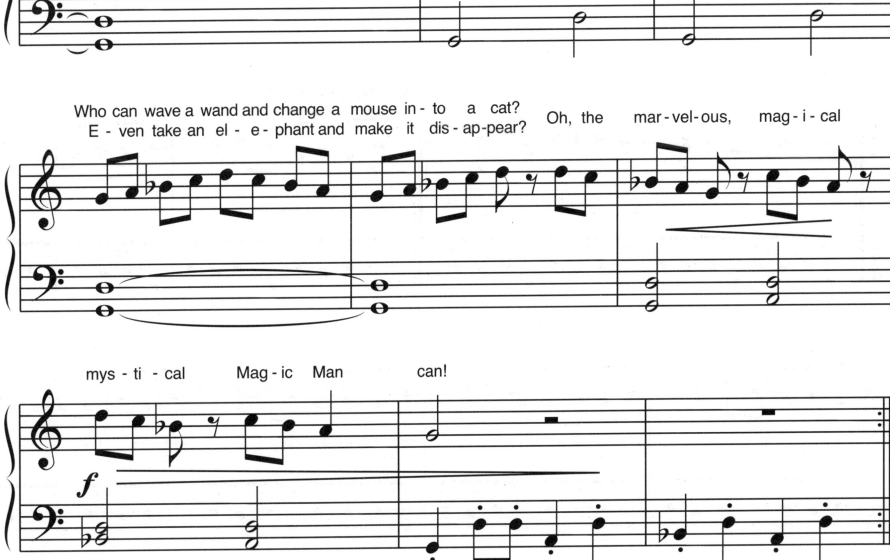

Freight Train

Play RH ONE OCTAVE LOWER.

Allegro Moderato

p poco a poco accelerando

(Start SLOWLY & SOFTLY. Gradually increase speed and volume, little by little, as the train gains speed.)

mf

1. Chug - gin' and a - huff - in',   roll - in' a - long!
2. Smok - in' and a - steam - in',   burn - in' up coal!

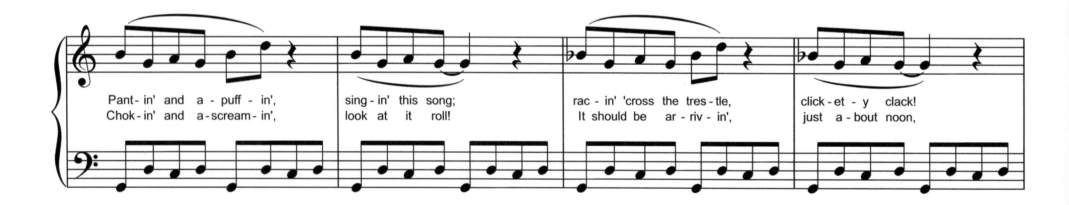

Pant - in' and a - puff - in',   sing - in' this song;   rac - in' 'cross the tres - tle,   click - et - y clack!
Chok - in' and a - scream - in',   look at it roll!   It should be ar - riv - in',   just a - bout noon,

AS WRITTEN (REGULAR RH G POSITION)

Lis - ten to the whis - tle
Whis - tlin' and a driv - in'

ech - o - in' back:
sing - in' this tune:

Woo, woo!
Woo, woo!

Woo, woo!
Woo, woo!

It's a
What a

(MOVE RH BACK TO OCTAVE LOWER.)   RH ONE OCTAVE LOWER.

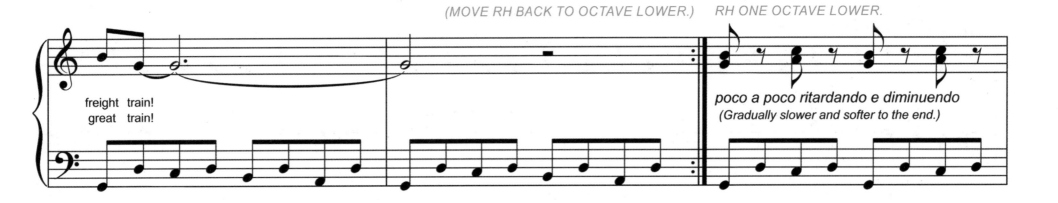

freight train!
great train!

poco a poco ritardando e diminuendo
(Gradually slower and softer to the end.)

Both hands
AS WRITTEN

The Greatest Show on Earth!

March Tempo

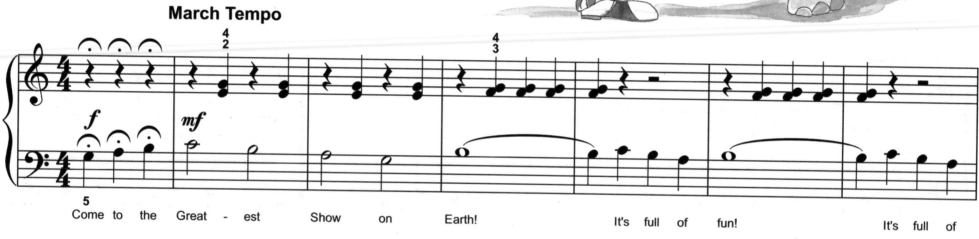

Come to the Great - est   Show   on   Earth!   It's full of fun!   It's full of

mirth!   Come see the clowns   and   tum - blers   too;   see what our   ac - ro -

bats can do! And when the mus - ic starts to play, you'll say "Hoo -

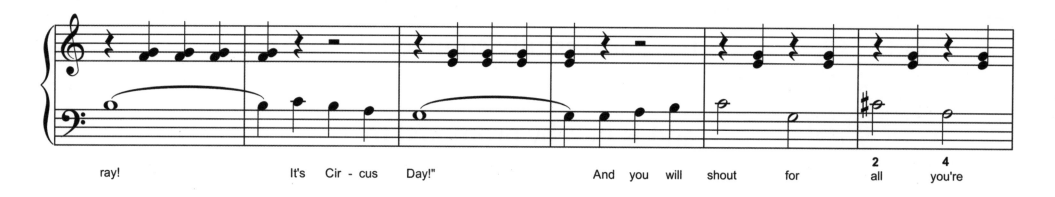

ray! It's Cir - cus Day!" And you will shout for all you're

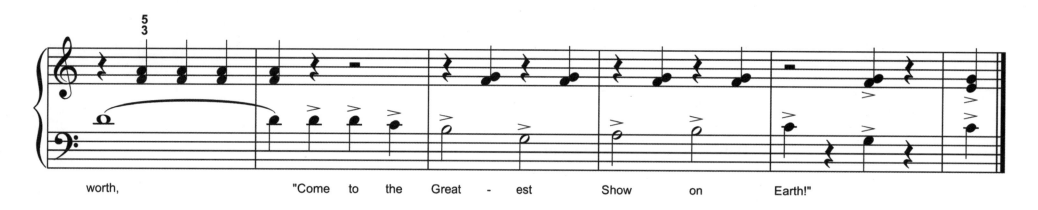

worth, "Come to the Great - est Show on Earth!"

Certificate of Promotion

This is to certify that

_____

has successfully completed

Alfred's Basic Graded Piano Course Book 1

and is hereby promoted to

Alfred's Basic Graded Piano Course Book 2

_____   _____
Date   Teacher